simply relevant

{ A TASTE OF FREEDOM }

Relational Bible Series *for Women*

STONECROFT® MINISTRIES

stonecroft.org

Group *for* Women

Loveland, Colorado

simply relevant

{ A TASTE OF FREEDOM }

Relational Bible Series for Women

Visit our website: **group.com/women**
www.stonecroft.org

Credits

Author: Linda Crawford
Executive Editor: Amy Nappa
Chief Creative Officer: Joani Schultz
Copy Editor: Amber Van Schooneveld and Ardeth Carlson
Print Production Artist: Eric Anderson
Art Director and Cover Designer: Andrea Filer
Senior Designer: Kari K. Monson
Production Manager: DeAnne Lear
Cover photography and photo on page 4 © 2009 Jupiterimages Corporation
Photos on pages 9, 10, 16, 19, 41, 42, 53, 54, 60, 65, and 66 © photos.com

ISBN 978-0-7644-4316-9
10 9 8 7 6 5 4 3 2 1   18 17 16 15 14 13 12 11 10 09
Printed in the United States of America

Contents

Welcome to Simply Relevant: A Taste of Freedom! This is your totally relevant six-week Bible series that will help you develop relationships with other women as you grow in your relationship with God.

OK, so what's a Bible series got to do with *a taste of freedom*, you ask? Well, this series is all about developing the spiritual fruit of self-control in our lives. And when we grow in this area, we experience freedom in a new way. Trust us! You're going to taste freedom like never before!

This flavor-themed Bible series also gives women who aren't quite convinced about coming to a church activity that extra little nudge to come. Paul's words, "I try to find common ground with everyone, doing everything I can to save some" (1 Corinthians 9:22) have never tasted so delicious. Reach out and find that common ground!

Each week, you'll taste a different aspect of God's goodness and learn how to develop the fruit of self-control in your life. You'll savor the sweetness of God's love, experience the richness of being resolute, explore how to make better (rather than bitter) choices, learn how to follow God's will when candy (or something else) tempts you, and nourish your dreams for a happy and healthy life of freedom! Whew! That's a long list, so we've given you bite-sized portions to digest to deepen and enrich your learning in a way you can really understand.

You can do this Bible series with five to 50 women—or even more! And you want women to really grow in relationships with each other, so always form small groups of four or five for discussion if you have a larger group. Women at any place in their faith journeys can feel right at home with this Bible series. The discussion questions can be understood and applied by women who don't know Jesus yet or women who are long-time friends with him. All the Bible passages are printed out for you, so those who aren't familiar with the Bible have the verses right in front of them.

So what will you be doing each week? Here's the structure of the sessions:

Note to the Hostess

Your hostess will be the woman facilitating your Bible series. She'll read the session through before the meeting, prepare for the activities, gather any supplies needed, and get the snacks ready. The "Note to the Hostess" box in each session contains special tips just for the hostess, such as supplies to gather, atmosphere to create, and ideas for snacks.

Mingling

Each week, you're going to start with snacks, mingling, and a short prayer. This is key: Take time to share how you did with your previous week's commitment.

Experience

Each week you'll engage in an experience that will bring a new depth of meaning to the topic you'll explore. The experiences will get every woman involved and having fun. There might be a little bit of preparation or supplies needed, which the hostess will supply.

The Word

Each week, you'll read a Scripture passage together and then discuss what it means with questions from this guide. The questions are surprising, personal, and relevant to women today.

A Closer Look

This is a quick look at the Bible passages you'll be digging into each week. They'll help you develop a deeper understanding of the verses at hand while discussing their meaning in your lives.

Take Action

This is where women put faith into action. You'll all commit to apply what you've learned in the coming week in a practical way. You can write your own commitment or choose from the suggested commitments. Then next week you'll check in with each other to see how you did.

Prayer

At the end of each session, you'll spend time in prayer together. You can ask for prayer requests and also pray about the commitments you've made for the upcoming week. We've also given you a verse to read together to focus your minds for prayer.

Girlfriend Time

If you want some more hangout time together after your session is over, we've given you fun suggestions for easy activities to do together to reinforce the session's topic or to just relax. This is an optional bonus that will help you grow deeper in your friendships.

Still Thirsty?

If you want to explore the week's topic more, we've given you additional verses and reflection questions to read and consider in the coming week.

We pray that in the next six weeks, this experience will help you grow as friends of Jesus and each other, and discover that the freedom of the fruit of self-control tastes even better than chocolate!

Music is a great tool in creating ambiance for your meeting area. Play music before and after your gathering. We recommend the *Music of Sweet Life Café*, which features songs related to many of the themes you'll explore in this Bible study. You can find it at group.com or at your local Christian bookstore.

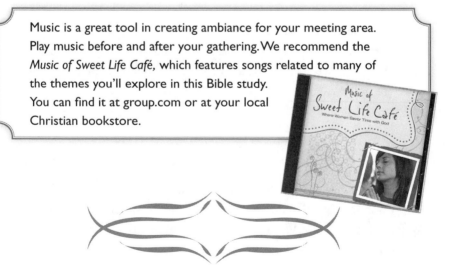

Taste and See

Self-control Tastes Good!

Note to the Hostess:

It's time for women to taste and see that the Lord is good! Many women struggle with issues of self-control and may feel vulnerable and self-conscious about attending this study. Make them feel safe by creating a warm and welcoming environment. Consider a less formal arrangement of tables and chairs in your room by creating small groups of four. Or use someone's living room or a room with more of a coffee-house feel to encourage deeper discussions.

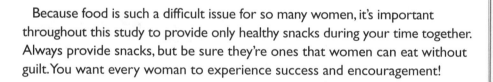

Because food is such a difficult issue for so many women, it's important throughout this study to provide only healthy snacks during your time together. Always provide snacks, but be sure they're ones that women can eat without guilt. You want every woman to experience success and encouragement!

Get It...Got It?...Good.

- ○ table with healthy snacks as described in the Experience section
- ○ table with pictures of tempting foods as described in the Experience section
- ○ slips of paper with titles of foods pictured

Mingling

Get women connected and help them feel comfortable right away by creating a relaxed atmosphere that's welcoming and supportive. Some women may be self-conscious about attending a study on self-control, so be sure to give them a personal welcome and help them to get introduced to other women. You'll enjoy snacks during your Experience time together, so use the mingling time for introductions and conversation starters.

Need a little help? Here's a conversation starter to try:

*Hi, my name's [your name],
and my favorite flavor is [_____].*

Before starting, pray something like this:

God, thank you for bringing each woman here tonight. Help us to discover how good it can be to taste the fruit of self-control and the joy of living in the freedom you have promised us. Amen.

Experience

(Note: The hostess will prepare this experience.) Many women struggle with self-control issues related to food. Do this activity to help them experience a taste of God's freedom in their lives.

Set up your snack area with two tables. On one table, instead of real food, display large *pictures* of tempting foods like pizza, ice cream, chocolates, cake, pies, cookies, cheesecake, muffins, and hamburgers with fries. (You can easily find pictures like these in magazines or on the internet.) In front of each picture provide several copies of printed slips of paper with the title of the item. (Several women may select the same strip so you'll need more than one of each.)

On the other table, offer healthy foods like a raw veggie tray, low-fat dips, unbuttered popcorn, sugar-free candy, and a large display of sliced fruit.

Tell women to go to each table and choose the snacks they would like to have. Tell them to choose as much as they would *really like* from each table. (They will take real food from the healthy table and slips of paper from the tempting table.)

After everyone has chosen snacks, discuss the following questions:

Q: How did you feel when choosing snack items from each table?

Q: How honest were you in the choices you made? What did you really want but didn't choose? Tell about that.

Q: If there had been real food on both tables, how would this experience have been different for you? How would that have changed the choices you made? the way you feel?

the Word

Have someone read Psalm 34:8-10 and John 8:34-36 aloud.

Psalm 34:8-10

Taste and see that the Lord is good. Oh, the joys of those who take refuge in him. Fear the Lord, you his godly people, for those who fear him will have all they need. Even strong young lions sometimes go hungry, but those who trust in the Lord will lack no good thing.

John 8:34-36

Jesus replied, "I tell you the truth, everyone who sins is a slave of sin. A slave is not a permanent member of the family, but a son is part of the family forever. So if the Son sets you free, you are truly free."

a closer look

Read this box anytime to take a deeper look at the verses for this session.

Some say "seeing is believing," but God instructs us to "taste and see" that he is good. What's that really mean? Just like we can't taste, savor, or enjoy pictures of delicious foods, we can't just look at God and know he's good. We must *experience* his goodness—tasting it, savoring it, and enjoying it!

Tasting of the Lord's goodness is like eating the healthiest foods possible for our bodies. They may not always be the sweetest tasting, but they're the nourishment we need to be the healthiest we can be. But wait—what about chocolate? our favorite ice cream? those wonderful french fries? If we taste those things, is it bad?

No. And God doesn't tell us to label foods "good" or "bad." In fact, Romans 14:14 says: **"I know and am convinced on the authority of the Lord Jesus that no food, in and of itself, is wrong to eat."** The food is not really the issue. But our appetites are. Most of us have experienced how easily a little self-indulgence can lead to a lot. Losing self-control leads us to sin and separates us from the goodness of God. But Jesus told us we're not to be slaves to our sin, because there's freedom—not the freedom to choose what the world gives us but a *true* freedom we can receive only from him. It's a freedom that tastes good and is good for us!

tasty tip

Self-control is identified in Galatians chapter 5 as a "fruit" that the work of the Spirit of God produces in us. Although we'd certainly prefer for God to *quickly* change out-of-control to self-control, it's clear from the Bible that growing and producing this fruit takes time. So it's important for us to keep in mind the steps a gardener would take to grow fruit—preparing the soil, sowing seeds, watering and tending, pruning and nurturing, and finally…harvesting. In this first session, allow God to help you prepare the soil of your heart and sow the seeds of his truth and love so your fruit will start to grow!

simply relevant | A TASTE OF FREEDOM   13

scripture discussion questions

In groups of four or five, discuss these questions:

Q: What are things, other than food, that a person might have self-control issues with?

Q: How do you think a person can "taste" and experience God's goodness?

Q: Imagine the two snack tables set up with one table to see the Lord's goodness and one to *taste* the Lord's goodness. What items would you put on each table?

Q: What do you think it means in Psalm 34 when it says, "Even strong young lions sometimes go hungry, but those who trust in the Lord will lack no good thing"?

Q: In control or out of control? captive or free? When it comes to self-control, how would you describe yourself right now?

Q: What's one goal you have for yourself with this Bible study?

Take Action

Let's not just *talk* about discovering how self-control can taste good, *let's do it!* Write below how you're going to taste and see the freedom and goodness of the Lord in the next week. If you're having a hard time thinking of something, choose one of the ideas below. Next week, you'll share with one another how you did.

this week

○ I'm going to taste and see that the Lord is good by:

....

....

....

....

○ I commit to sitting down and writing out an honest list of all the areas in my life that are out of control. Then I'll have a long talk with God about them.

○ This week, when I am tempted by something that I know is not God's best for me, I will admit my weakness of self-control to God. Then I'll pray for the strength to stay connected to the freedom from sin I have as a part of his family.

○ Each time I find myself feeling guilty for failures of self-control, I'll stop and remember God's goodness. Then I'll choose to do something that's healthy and that I can feel good about. (Smiling is a great way to start!)

Prayer

End your time together in prayer to your Father.
Read Romans 14:17 together:

> For the Kingdom of God is not a matter of what we eat or drink, but of living a life of goodness and peace and joy in the Holy Spirit.

God knows we struggle with self-control. Too often we make the issue the focus instead of God. His greatest desire is that we would stay focused on him so we can experience his goodness, rest in his peace, and be filled with his joy! Ask God to help you to taste and see his goodness and nourish you with his love. Thank him for developing the fruit of self-control in your life and for the freedom from sin he has promised you.

Girlfriend Time

Take time to share stories of God's goodness in your lives. Form small groups of four, and share about times in your life when you thought "Wow! God is good!" or felt like God was really doing something wonderful.

And remember, this is a journey taken one step at a time. Step one for today is a smile and a hug of encouragement. Make time for it right now!

Still Thirsty?

If you're still thirsty to know more, check out these Scriptures.

Galatians 5:22-23

"But the Holy Spirit produces this kind of fruit in our lives: love, joy, peace, patience, kindness, goodness, faithfulness, gentleness, and self-control. There is no law against these things!"

Q: Why do you think self-control is included here? Why do you think having self-control could be as important as having love or kindness?

1 Corinthians 10:23

"You say, 'I am allowed to do anything'—but not everything is good for you. You say, 'I am allowed to do anything'—but not everything is beneficial."

Q: What's the difference between the freedom we have in the world and the freedom we experience as a part of the family of God? How can God help you to make choices that are beneficial to you?

Matthew 6:25-27

"That is why I tell you not to worry about everyday life—whether you have enough food and drink, or enough clothes to wear. Isn't life more than food, and your body more than clothing? Look at the birds. They don't plant or harvest or store food in barns, for your heavenly Father feeds them. And aren't you far more valuable to him than they are? Can all your worries add a single moment to your life?"

Q: How can worry play a part in a lack of self-control? How can trusting God for all your needs help you develop more self-control in your life?

Romans 7:14-25

"So the trouble is not with the law, for it is spiritual and good. The trouble is with me, for I am all too human, a slave to sin. I don't really understand myself, for I want to do what is right, but I don't do it. Instead, I do what I hate. But if I know that what I am doing is wrong, this shows that I agree that the law is good. So I am not the one doing wrong; it is sin living in me that does it.

And I know that nothing good lives in me, that is, in my sinful nature I want to do what is right, but I can't. I want to do what is good, but I don't. I don't want to do what is wrong, but I do it anyway. But if I do what I don't want to do, I am not really the one doing wrong; it is sin living in me that does it.

I have discovered this principle of life—that when I want to do what is right, I inevitably do what is wrong. I love God's law with all my heart. But there is another power within me that is at war with my mind. This power makes me a slave to the sin that is still within me. Oh, what a miserable person I am! Who will free me from this life that is dominated by sin and death? Thank God! The answer is in Jesus Christ our Lord."

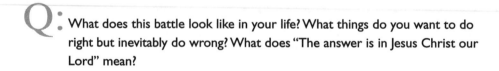

Q: What does this battle look like in your life? What things do you want to do right but inevitably do wrong? What does "The answer is in Jesus Christ our Lord" mean?

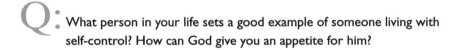

Philippians 3:17-21

"Dear brothers and sisters, pattern your lives after mine, and learn from those who follow our example. For I have told you often before, and I say it again with tears in my eyes, that there are many whose conduct shows they are really enemies of the cross of Christ. They are headed for destruction. Their god is their appetite, they brag about shameful things, and they think only about this life here on earth. But we are citizens of heaven, where the Lord Jesus Christ lives. And we are eagerly waiting for him to return as our Savior. He will take our weak mortal bodies and change them into glorious bodies like his own, using the same power with which he will bring everything under his control."

Q: What person in your life sets a good example of someone living with self-control? How can God give you an appetite for him?

My Reflections

Bitter or Better?

Making Spirit-Led Choices

Note to the Hostess:

We make so many choices in a day. Some are simple with small consequences (like what to wear). Others are more complex and can have larger consequences (like what we say and do). What happens when self-led control of our choices leads to out-of-control? How can we develop God-led self-control in our lives that restores our hope and sweetens our lives?

This week women will explore the difference between *Spirit-led* self-control and *self-led* self-control. Many times we can become bitter and discouraged in our quest for healthy self-control in our lives. Things may not always turn out the way we want, even when we do our best to follow God's leading. Other times things turn out poorly because we've made choices based on our own desires—ones that we know were not pleasing to God. In this session women will take an honest look at their attitude about the fruit of self-control and seek to let the Spirit of God gain control of the choices they make.

Get It...Got It?...Good.

- healthy snacks such as fruit, vegetables, or granola bars and something tasty to drink
- tables for Experience section
- for each group of four:
  - 2 plates (disposable foam ones with a ridge around the edge work well)
  - red, blue, and green food coloring
  - about a cup of fat-free milk
  - 1 spoon
  - dish detergent in small squeeze bottles

Mingling

Before you enjoy your healthy snacks, pray something like this:

Thank you, God, for the opportunity we have to share faith and friendships together today. The desire of our hearts is to live a life that is pleasing to you. Help the fruit of self-control ripen within us as we study together and spend time with you. In Jesus' name we pray, amen.

As the women eat, encourage them to share about the Take Action commitments they made last week. Use these questions as discussion starters:

Q: How did you practice tasting and seeing God's goodness in your life?

Q: What difference did it make?

Experience (Part 1)

(Note: The hostess will prepare this experience.) Is *self-control* just another name for willpower? What happens when we depend on ourselves to be in control? Do this activity to help women experience the different consequences of self-led and Spirit-led choices.

Have women form small groups of four at a table. Give each group a plate, about half a cup of fat-free milk, a spoon, and small bottles of red, blue, and green food coloring. Tell them to pour the milk onto the plate, and use the food coloring and the spoon to make something very colorful. The person with the spoon should stir often.

After each group has completed this activity, have them discuss the following questions:

Q: How would you describe the mixture on your plate?

Q: Did your activity turn out the way you wanted it to? What could have been better?

Experience (Part 2)

It's time to try this again, but with a twist! For part 2 of the Experience, each group should follow these specific instructions:

1. Use a clean plate, and pour about half a cup of milk onto the plate.

2. Do not bump, stir, or jiggle the plate at any time during the activity.

3. Place three small drops of each color in one spot, an equal distance from each other along the outside edge of the milk. There should be only three dots of color in the milk.

4. Have one person drip a small amount of detergent in the center of the plate.

5. Wait and watch!

Give women time to watch and comment on how the colors are mixing on the second plate. Then discuss these questions:

Q: Which activity had the better outcome, and why?

Q: How is this like or unlike following God's instructions for our lives?

Q: How can this experiment illustrate what happens when we depend on the Spirit of God to direct us?

the Word

Read Romans 8:1-9 together.

Romans 8:1-9

So now there is no condemnation for those who belong to Christ Jesus. And because you belong to him, the power of the life-giving Spirit has freed you from the power of sin that leads to death. The law of Moses was unable to save us because of the weakness of our sinful nature. So God did what the law could not do. He sent his own Son in a body like the bodies we sinners have. And in that body God declared an end to sin's control over us by giving his Son as a sacrifice for our sins. He did this so that the just requirement of the law would be fully satisfied for us, who no longer follow our sinful nature but instead follow the Spirit.

Those who are dominated by the sinful nature think about sinful things, but those who are controlled by the Holy Spirit think about things that please the Spirit. So letting your sinful nature control your mind leads to death. But letting the Spirit control your mind leads to life and peace. For the sinful nature is always hostile to God. It never did obey God's laws, and it never will. That's why those who are still under the control of their sinful nature can never please God.

But you are not controlled by your sinful nature. You are controlled by the Spirit if you have the Spirit of God living in you.

a closer look

Read this box anytime to take a deeper look at the verses for this session.

This week's Scripture contains the very strong statement that letting our sinful nature control our mind will lead to death. But there's also a promise that the power of the life-giving Spirit has freed us from the power of sin that leads to death. What's it all mean?

Let's think about the freedom of choice we have in life. We are free to make choices based on whatever we want. Yet the biggest choice we are making is whether or not to be in a relationship with God. A person who has chosen to reject God is therefore cut off from God and doesn't have the power of God in her life to give her direction. But the person who chooses a relationship with God enjoys life and peace, even in the midst of external turmoil.

Scripture is very clear that the choices we make without God are not the best choices for our lives. But with Jesus in our lives, we have the power of the Spirit of God to help us *overcome* sinful desires. We can ask God to help us make choices that lead to life and peace.

So instead of feeling discouraged and bitter, we can believe God for something better. Instead of always wanting, we can trust God to provide what we need. And instead of accepting defeat over our struggles with self-led self-control, we can surrender to the control of the Spirit in our lives.

scripture discussion questions

In groups of four or five, discuss these questions:

Q: What do you think the passage "the sinful nature is always hostile to God" means? How have you experienced that in your own life?

Q: How does a person become more Spirit-led and less self-led when it comes to self-control?

Q: According to this passage, is self-control the same as willpower? Why or why not?

Q: Things don't always turn out the way we want—even when we've done our best to make Spirit-led choices. How can we avoid becoming bitter and keep believing for something better?

tasty tip

Think about how you would describe the taste of the fruit of the Spirit. What would love taste like? joy? goodness? They sound like they'd be sweet, don't they?

What about self-control? sweet, bitter, or just plain yucky? Maybe to you self-control is like a piece of unsweetened chocolate—it looks like it should taste good, but after you try it you just want to spit it out!

Here's a tip—fruits don't get sweet on their own—they need the sun to ripen them. A green plum is bitter. But give it enough sun, and it will eventually turn sweet!

It's the same for the fruit of the Spirit you're trying to grow. If the fruit of self-control isn't sweet tasting in your life yet, try spending more time with Jesus, and let it ripen up in the Son-shine!

Take Action

Let's not just *talk* about discovering how to make Spirit-led choices of self-control, *let's do it!* Write below how you're going to trade any bitter impressions you have about the fruit of self-control for the better taste of living with the power of the Spirit of God in your life. If you're having a hard time thinking of something, choose one of the ideas below. Next week, you'll share with one another how you did.

this week

○ I commit to making an effort to make more Spirit-led choices by:

....

....

....

....

○ I will take time this week to pray and ask God before I make choices.

○ I will examine my attitudes about the fruit of self-control and honestly admit if I feel bitter, angry, discouraged, or hopeless. Then I'll pray and ask God to replace those attitudes with joy.

○ To help the fruit of self-control ripen to sweetness in my life, I commit to spending more time with Jesus and living in his Son-shine.

Prayer

End your time together in prayer to your Father.
Read Galatians 5:25 together:

> *Since we are living by the Spirit, let us follow the Spirit's leading in every part of our lives.*

God never lets go of us. He is always there to guide us to the abundant life he has promised us. Pray for God to strengthen you and help you seek and follow his leading in every part of your life. Ask for his guidance to make Spirit-led choices that will help the fruit of self-control grow and ripen in your life.

Girlfriend Time

At the end of your study, have women return to view the plates and talk about how the colors have changed or not changed over time. Let women add detergent to the first plate to see what happens. How is this similar to asking God to fix up a mess we made on our own?

Still Thirsty?

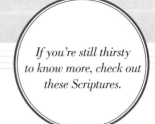

If you're still thirsty to know more, check out these Scriptures.

Galatians 5:16-18

"So I say, let the Holy Spirit guide your lives. Then you won't be doing what your sinful nature craves. The sinful nature wants to do evil, which is just the opposite of what the Spirit wants. And the Spirit gives us desires that are the opposite of what the sinful nature desires. These two forces are constantly fighting each other, so you are not free to carry out your good intentions. But when you are directed by the Spirit, you are not under obligation to the law of Moses."

Q: What does this fight of opposing desires look like in your life? How can the spiritual desires win?

Mark 8:34-37

"Then, calling the crowd to join his disciples, he said, 'If any of you wants to be my follower, you must turn from your selfish ways, take up your cross, and follow me. If you try to hang on to your life, you will lose it. But if you give up your life for my sake and for the sake of the Good News, you will save it. And what do you benefit if you gain the whole world but lose your soul? Is anything worth more than your soul?'"

Q: How can "selfish ways" hinder us from leading a life of Spirit-led self-control? How do we "give up our life" to find true life?

Galatians 6:8

"Those who live only to satisfy their own sinful nature will harvest decay and death from that sinful nature. But those who live to please the Spirit will harvest everlasting life from the Spirit."

Q: What choices do you make that are to please yourself? What changes can you make to please the Spirit and harvest life?

Mark 4:3-8

"Listen! A farmer went out to plant some seed. As he scattered it across his field, some of the seed fell on a footpath, and the birds came and ate it. Other seed fell on shallow soil with underlying rock. The seed sprouted quickly because the soil was shallow. But the plant soon wilted under the hot sun, and since it didn't have deep roots, it died. Other seed fell among thorns that grew up and choked out the tender plants so they produced no grain. Still other seeds fell on fertile soil, and they sprouted, grew, and produced a crop that was thirty, sixty, and even a hundred times as much as had been planted!"

Q: God desires for us to develop the fruit of self-control in our lives. Using the examples in this passage, can you identify things that are hindering the seeds of self-control from growing in your life?

When the Refrigerator Calls

Finding Protection in God's Will

Note to the Hostess:

Candy is so tempting—because it tastes so good! But eating too much will make us sick. Losing self-control and giving in to temptations in other areas of our lives can make us sick, too. To stay healthy, we need God-given self-control so we know how much is too much and when to say "yes," "no," and "not now."

Candy is tempting…and you'll be using actual candy in your activity time together this week. But you won't be tempted to eat it after you're done! So be prepared for an experience that's a little serious and a lot messy. Laugh and have fun together as you discover how following God's will can protect you from temptation.

Get It…Got It?…Good.

- healthy snacks such as fruit, granola, and veggies. Remember to offer something good to drink as well.
- individually wrapped chocolate pieces (such as Hershey's Kisses)
- wet wipes

Mingling

Before starting, give women time to enjoy the healthy snacks and talk about their week.

Use these questions as discussion starters:

Q: How were you able to make more Spirit-led self-controlled choices this week?

Q: How are your attitudes about self-control changing?

Before starting, pray something like this:

Thank you, God, for the fruit of self-control you are developing in our lives. Continue to teach us your will, and strengthen our faith to help us make wise choices in our lives. In Jesus' name, amen.

Experience

(Note: The hostess will prepare this experience.) We can be tempted by desires for food, wealth, success, physical pleasure, and entertainment. Anything that tempts us to make choices outside God's will for our lives tests the fruit of self-control. Do this activity to help women experience the reality and consequences of dealing with temptations.

Give each woman a wrapped piece of chocolate (such as a Hershey's Kiss).

Have everyone unwrap the piece and place it in the open palm of her hand. Next, ask women to look at the candy and think of it as something in their lives that tempts them to lose self-control. It could be food, TV, shopping, gossip, or another area they're asking God to help them with. When they have that temptation in mind, have them close their fingers tightly around the chocolate, and have them hold it closed until you tell them to let go (about 3 minutes).

While they are holding the chocolate, read:

Proverbs 25:28

"A person without self-control is like a city with broken-down walls."

Have women discuss these questions with the person sitting next to them:

Q: What does this verse mean?

Q: What could help you build stronger walls of protection to resist future temptations?

After about 3 or 4 minutes of discussion, have women open their hands and look at the (now melted) chocolate. Discuss:

Q: Has the appeal of the candy changed for you? Why or why not?

Q: When we choose to give in to temptation and, in essence, grasp it and hold onto it, what happens? How does this compare with the chocolate on your hand?

Use wet wipes to clean off hands, and continue the discussion:

Q: How does God help us wipe away the results of our sinful choices?

the Word

Read Matthew 4:1-11 together.

Matthew 4:1-11

Then Jesus was led by the Spirit into the wilderness to be tempted there by the devil. For forty days and forty nights he fasted and became very hungry. During that time the devil came and said to him, "If you are the Son of God, tell these stones to become loaves of bread." But Jesus told him, "No! The Scriptures say, 'People do not live by bread alone, but by every word that comes from the mouth of God.'

Then the devil took him to the holy city, Jerusalem, to the highest point of the Temple, and said, "If you are the Son of God, jump off! For the Scriptures say, 'He will order his angels to protect you. And they will hold you up with their hands so you won't even hurt your foot on a stone.' " Jesus responded, "The Scriptures also say, 'You must not test the Lord your God.' "

Next the devil took him to the peak of a very high mountain and showed him all the kingdoms of the world and their glory. "I will give it all to you," he said, "if you will kneel down and worship me." "Get out of here, Satan," Jesus told him. "For the Scriptures say, 'You must worship the Lord your God and serve only him.' "

Then the devil went away, and angels came and took care of Jesus.

a closer look

Read this box anytime to take a deeper look at the verses for this session.

Jesus was without sin or imperfection, yet immediately after his baptism and before he began his earthly ministry, the Holy Spirit led him into the wilderness to be tempted by Satan. To be tempted just as we are tempted. To prove that no matter what, he would choose the path God had planned. It was a necessary step in strengthening him for the journey to the cross that lay ahead.

Temptations that come into our lives have the potential to strengthen us for the journey ahead, too. They are a test of whether we will choose to live for God or for our earthly desires. A test of Spirit-led self-control over self-led self-control.

Being tempted does not mean we have moral failures or weaknesses. Jesus was perfect, but he was still tempted. It's what we do in the face of temptation that's what matters.

So what's the best way to deal with temptation? Study what Jesus did, and then do what he did. With God's will, God's Word, and God's presence, temptations can help you become the strong and mighty woman of God he wants you to be!

scripture discussion questions

In groups of four or five, discuss these questions:

Q: What were the three specific ways the devil tried to tempt Jesus? Which of these temptations have you experienced in your own life?

Q: What can we learn for our own lives from the ways Jesus resisted temptation?

Q: Jesus said, "People do not live by bread alone, but by every word that comes from the mouth of God." How can Scripture be like food to us? How can it help strengthen our walls to resist temptation?

Q: The devil came to tempt Jesus when he was alone in the wilderness. When are you the most vulnerable to temptation? How can a change in environment help you resist temptation?

Q: What are three areas of temptation in your life right now? What Scriptures can you use to help you resist those temptations?

tasty tip

Imagine how hungry Jesus must have been after not eating for forty days! He had the ability to turn stones into bread, but he refused to use his power to feed himself. Why? Because the devil was not really tempting Jesus to satisfy his hunger. He was tempting him to act independently of God's perfect will.

Satan tried to tempt Eve the same way by putting doubt in her mind about God's will:

"Did God really say you must not eat the fruit from any of the trees in the garden?" (Genesis 3:1)

Jesus was able to resist temptation because he knew exactly what God's will for him was. Eve wasn't so sure, so doubt and unbelief made her more vulnerable.

What tips can we learn from them for dealing with temptation in our own lives?

Take Action

Let's not just *talk* about discovering how to resist temptation, *let's do it!* Write below how you're going to seek God's will and strengthen your ability to resist temptation through Godly self-control in the next week. If you're having a hard time thinking of something, choose one of the ideas below. Next week, you'll share with one another how you did.

this week

○ I'm going to seek to know God's will for my life by:

....

....

....

....

○ I commit to making a list of three areas of temptation in my life and finding Bible verses I can use to help me resist those temptations.

○ This week, I will admit any doubt or unbelief I have to God and pray for him to strengthen my faith to believe his promises for my life.

○ When I face temptation this week, I'll think about what happened when I held the chocolate in my hand and remember that choosing my will over God's just makes a mess!

Prayer

End your time together in prayer to your Father.
Read Hebrews 4:15-16 together:

> This High Priest of ours understands our weaknesses, for he faced all of the same testings we do, yet he did not sin. So let us come boldly to the throne of our gracious God. There we will receive his mercy, and we will find grace to help us when we need it most.

So many times we feel alone in our struggles with temptation and self-control. But we are never alone. Even when other people in our lives can't understand, Jesus does. He's been tempted the same way we are. So it's important for us to come to him and ask for his mercy and grace when we need it most. Pray for God's presence and his will for your life when you face temptation this week.

Girlfriend Time

This week's study is a challenging and thought-provoking one, so take time to unwind! Shift the focus from temptations to something that is God's perfect will for every woman—joy!

"The joy of the Lord is your strength!" (Nehemiah 8:10)

Play a game that leads to lots of laughter, put on a silly skit, or watch a funny video together. Have fun!

Strengthen the walls of your faith with joy!

Still Thirsty?

If you're still thirsty to know more, check out these Scriptures.

John 4:31-34

"Meanwhile, the disciples were urging Jesus, 'Rabbi, eat something.' But Jesus replied, 'I have a kind of food you know nothing about.'

" 'Did someone bring him food while we were gone?' the disciples asked each other. Then Jesus explained: 'My nourishment comes from doing the will of God, who sent me, and from finishing his work.' "

Q: When faced with temptation, how can choosing to do God's will nourish and satisfy you? How can sharing God's love with another person feed your spirit?

Proverbs 20:17

"Stolen bread tastes sweet, but it turns to gravel in the mouth."

Q: What does this Scripture mean to you? What "sweet thing" has tempted you recently but then turned to gravel?

Genesis 32:24-31

"This left Jacob all alone in the camp, and a man came and wrestled with him until the dawn began to break. When the man saw that he would not win the match, he touched Jacob's hip and wrenched it out of its socket. Then the man said, 'Let me go, for the dawn is breaking!' But Jacob said, 'I will not let you go unless you bless me.'

" 'What is your name?' the man asked. He replied, 'Jacob.' 'Your name will no longer be Jacob,' the man told him. 'From now on you will be called Israel, because you have fought with God and with men and have won.'

" 'Please tell me your name,' Jacob said. 'Why do you want to know my name?' the man replied. Then he blessed Jacob there.

"Jacob named the place Peniel (which means 'face of God'), for he said, 'I have seen God face to face, yet my life has been spared.' The sun was rising as Jacob left Peniel, and he was limping because of the injury to his hip."

Q: How is Jacob's wrestling match with God similar to how our wills wrestle with God's will? How would having a "limp" help us to discover God's will in our lives? When wrestling with temptation how can we hold onto God until we receive our blessing?

Ecclesiastes 6:9

"Enjoy what you have rather than desiring what you don't have. Just dreaming about nice things is meaningless—like chasing the wind."

Q: What "nice things" do you dream about? How can dreaming lead to temptation in your life? If you were able to enjoy what you had, how would it help you with self-control?

1 Timothy 6:6-10

"Yet true godliness with contentment is itself great wealth. After all, we brought nothing with us when we came into the world, and we can't take anything with us when we leave it. So if we have enough food and clothing, let us be content.

"But people who long to be rich fall into temptation and are trapped by many foolish and harmful desires that plunge them into ruin and destruction. For the love of money is the root of all kinds of evil. And some people, craving money, have wandered from the true faith and pierced themselves with many sorrows."

Q: What longings for possessions in your life have led to harmful desires? How have temptations for material wealth led to a loss of faith in your life? destruction? sorrow? How can you avoid these temptations and desire instead to become rich in contentment?

Spicy or Sweet?

Savoring the Sweetness of God's Love

Note to the Hostess:

Create an atmosphere this week that makes women feel loved and special. Use candles, flowers, soft music, white table-cloths—you can even break out the good china!

Help every woman feel like a V.I.G. (Very Important Girlfriend) by welcoming each one as an honored guest. Be sure to read the Experience and Girlfriend Time sections to help you prepare for your time together.

Get It...Got It?...Good.

- healthy snacks and something to drink
- tablecloths, flowers, soft music, and candles
- whole strawberries
- plastic knives and toothpicks
- pampering activities for Girlfriend Time

Mingling

Before starting, give women time to enjoy the healthy snacks and talk about their week. Use these questions as discussion starters:

Q: How did you use Scripture to help you with self-control this week?

Q: Last week we discussed Proverbs 25:28: "A person without self-control is like a city with broken-down walls." How are your walls being strengthened through this study?

Before starting, pray something like this:

Thank you, God, for loving us so much that you sacrificed your Son so we may have eternal life with you. Open our hearts and fill us with your love so we may live every day in the knowledge of the power and beauty of your love for us. In Jesus' name, amen.

Experience

(Note: The hostess will prepare this experience.) This activity lets everyone experience how important it is to keep their hearts filled with God's love to develop the fruit of self-control.

Have each woman take a whole strawberry, four toothpicks, and a plastic knife. Explain that each strawberry represents a heart, and hearts can be fragile. Ask each woman to think about something that has happened in her past that hurt her heart.

Then have women cut their strawberries in half from top to bottom with the plastic knife to represent that hurt. Take a few minutes to discuss the following question in pairs.

Q: How can a wounded heart influence us to make choices that are not God's best for our lives?

After a few minutes tell the women that we all have experienced things that hurt our hearts, but when we accept Jesus, God is able to give us a new heart. Read this Scripture:

Ezekiel 36:26-27

"And I will give you a new heart, and I will put a new spirit in you. I will take out your stony, stubborn heart and give you a tender, responsive heart. And I will put my Spirit in you so that you will follow my decrees and be careful to obey my regulations."

God wants to give each of us a new heart—one that is filled with his love. Put the two pieces of the strawberry back together using the four toothpicks so that the toothpicks form a cross in the middle of the strawberry. Read this Scripture:

Proverbs 4:23

"Guard your heart above all else, for it determines the course of your life."

In small groups, discuss:

Q: What does it mean to "guard your heart"?

Q: How do our hearts influence the course of our lives?

Q: God said that after he gave us a new heart he would "put my Spirit in you so that you will follow my decrees." How important is the condition of your heart in developing the fruit of self-control in your life?

the Word

Read Romans 8:38-39 together.

Romans 8:38-39

And I am convinced that nothing can ever separate us from God's love. Neither death nor life, neither angels nor demons, neither our fears for today nor our worries about tomorrow—not even the powers of hell can separate us from God's love. No power in the sky above or in the earth below—indeed, nothing in all creation will ever be able to separate us from the love of God that is revealed in Christ Jesus our Lord.

a closer look

Read this box anytime to take a deeper look at the verses for this session.

Nothing can separate us from God's love. Not worries, not fears, not wrong choices—not even guilt.

Guilt. It's a "g" word we sometimes give more power in our lives than the big "G"—God! We eat too much and feel guilty. We say angry words—and feel guilty. We buy things we can't afford—and feel guilty. We watch a movie we shouldn't—and feel guilty. We tell a lie to get what we want—and feel guilty.

Too ashamed to tell anyone, let alone talk to God about how we feel, we allow our hearts to fill up with remorse. Pretty soon it's hard to feel God's love for us. If we've struggled with an issue of self-control over a long period of time, we may have a hard time believing God even loves us anymore.

Guilt and shame can distract our thoughts away from God's great love for us and weaken our ability to live from a heart of love. If we think more about guilt than we do about God's love for us, we'll have a difficult time making Spirit-led choices in our lives. Instead of focusing on feelings of guilt we need to fill our hearts and minds with the knowledge of God's love for us. Because nothing can separate us from it.

God loves you. Right this very moment. God loved you all day yesterday and will love you all day tomorrow. Believe it. Because living a victorious life of self-control depends on living from a heart overflowing with his love.

scripture discussion questions

In groups of four or five, discuss these questions:

Q: How does guilt make it difficult to accept and believe in God's love for you?

Q: What's the relationship between having self-control and having hearts that are filled with God's love?

Q: How can we stay connected to the *knowledge* of God's love? How does that knowledge give us strength in the face of temptation?

Q: Do you believe in God's love for you? What makes it difficult for you to receive his love?

Q: Speaking the wrong words to another person can be hurtful. But what about the negative words we speak about ourselves? How do they harm us? What does it reveal about our hearts when we speak negatively about ourselves?

tasty tip

Matthew 12:34-35

"For whatever is in your heart determines what you say. A good person produces good things from the treasury of a good heart, and an evil person produces evil things from the treasury of an evil heart."

What we say is all about what's in our hearts. Are your words more spicy than sweet? Burning hot or soothing to the soul? The next time you're tempted to lose your cool, try taking a deep breath first, and fill the treasury of your heart with love before you speak. Those sweet words you'll say will taste so much better!

Take Action

Let's not just *talk* about discovering how to savor the sweetness of God's love, *let's do it!* Write below how you're going to fill your heart with God's love and seek to let your heart direct your choices in the next week. If you're having a hard time thinking of something, choose one of the ideas below. Next week, you'll share with one another how you did.

this week

○ I'm going savor the sweetness of God's love for me by:

....

....

....

....

○ I commit to making a list of things I feel guilty about and having an honest talk with God about them. Then I'll pray for God to replace the guilt with his love.

○ I will share positive words of affirmation with a girlfriend to help fill her heart with God's love.

○ When I struggle with controlling my words this week, I'll take a moment to fill my heart with the knowledge of God's love before I speak.

Prayer

Everything we do and say flows from what's in our hearts, so end your time together by praying this passage of Scripture: Psalm 19:14

> *May the words of my mouth and the meditation of my heart be pleasing to you, O Lord, my rock and my redeemer.*

God loved us so much, he sent his only Son to die for us. That's a great big, huge kind of love! And nothing can separate us from it! How desperately our bruised and wounded hearts need to be filled with his love. Pray that this week, God will fill our hearts with his love and help us learn to let our hearts guide us in everything we say and do.

Girlfriend Time

To end your evening together this week, take time to enjoy special pampering activities. Give each other hand massages, take time to paint your nails, or do simple facials. You are special to God and to your girlfriends!

Before the evening is over be sure you've taken time for hugs and to remind each other of your love for each other and of God's love for you. Just hearing "God loves you!" can be an encouragement.

Still Thirsty?

If you're still thirsty to know more, check out these Scriptures.

1 John 4:13-17

"And God has given us his Spirit as proof that we live in him and he in us. Furthermore, we have seen with our own eyes and now testify that the Father sent his Son to be the Savior of the world. All who confess that Jesus is the Son of God have God living in them, and they live in God. We know how much God loves us, and we have put our trust in his love. God is love, and all who live in love live in God, and God lives in them. And as we live in God, our love grows more perfect."

Q: What can you do to live more in God and in love? How can love help you be more self-controlled?

Matthew 6:19-21

"Don't store up treasures here on earth, where moths eat them and rust destroys them, and where thieves break in and steal. Store your treasures in heaven, where moths and rust cannot destroy, and thieves do not break in and steal. Wherever your treasure is, there the desires of your heart will also be."

Q: What treasures have you stored up on earth? Be honest. What are the desires of your heart right now? If your heart was filled with the treasures of God's love, how might your desires change?

Psalm 139:23-24

"Search me, O God, and know my heart; test me and know my anxious thoughts. Point out anything in me that offends you, and lead me along the path of everlasting life."

Q: Are you able to ask God to search your heart? How can you be more vulnerable with God? What might be the result?

Proverbs 3:5-6

"Trust in the Lord with all your heart; do not depend on your own understanding. Seek his will in all you do, and he will show you which path to take."

Q: What does it mean to trust the Lord with all your heart? How does this relate to self-control?

John 15:9-11

"I have loved you even as the Father has loved me. Remain in my love. When you obey my commandments, you remain in my love, just as I obey my Father's commandments and remain in his love. I have told you these things so that you will be filled with my joy."

Q: Nothing can separate us from God's love, but this passage indicates that obedience keeps us living in his love. What's the difference? How can making God-guided choices help us to "remain" in his love?

My Reflections

My Reflections

Flavors for Life

Recipe for Successful Self-control

Note to the Hostess:

This session you'll experience God's recipe for developing self-control and how rich and flavorful our lives can become when we follow that recipe!

To go with the theme of this session, decorate your area with aprons, cooking utensils, measuring cups, and cookbooks. You may want to set up a special area with extra spice and herb recipes women can copy to take home. Serve herb dip with fresh vegetables, and spiced yogurt dip with fresh fruit. Hot and cold herbal teas with fresh mint leaves will add to the rich flavor experience!

Get It...Got It?...Good.

- healthy snacks and something to drink as described above
- containers of dried spices
- measuring spoons
- small plastic bags
- herb seeds and starter pots for planting (optional)

Mingling

It's all about experiencing flavors and more flavors this week! During this fellowship time, encourage women to taste different herbal teas, enjoy the herb and spice dips, and explore the spices and recipes you have on display.

Use these discussion starters to help women talk about their week:

Q: Describe how you savored God's love for you this week.

Q: Share how successful you were at controlling your words and speaking from a heart of love.

Before starting, pray something like this:

Thank you, Lord, for your precious love for each woman here. May it fill our hearts and give life to our spirits. As we spend time together in your presence, help us to experience the richness of the abundant life Jesus promised us. Strengthen and encourage us as we persevere in cultivating the fruit of self-control in our lives. In Jesus' name, amen.

Experience

(Note: The hostess will prepare this experience.) It takes good recipes to create flavorful foods, and successful cooks know just the right ingredients to use and just the right steps to take. In this experience you'll consider the ingredients for a "recipe" God has given us to produce the fruit of self-control in our lives.

Form groups of four to six. Arrange an area for each group with the spices listed in the recipe, measuring spoons, and small plastic bags. Before they follow the recipe, have women smell each spice first and discuss the following question.

Q: How is each spice unique? How do herbs and spices enhance the flavors of our food?

Follow the recipe below to assemble your own spice blend in a plastic bag.

Recipe

Seven-Spice Mix

¾ tablespoon dried marjoram

¾ tablespoon dried thyme

¾ tablespoon dried savory

¼ teaspoon dried basil

¼ teaspoon dried rosemary

⅛ teaspoon dried sage

⅛ teaspoon fennel seeds

Mix all ingredients, and seal in bag. Use to season chicken, vegetables, or meat.

After women have assembled the spice mix, have them discuss:

Q: How does following a recipe help you? What does following a recipe require of us?

Read this Scripture:

Philippians 4:8-9

"And now, dear brothers and sisters, one final thing. Fix your thoughts on what is true, and honorable, and right, and pure, and lovely, and admirable. Think about things that are excellent and worthy of praise. Keep putting into practice all you learned and received from me—everything you heard from me and saw me doing. Then the God of peace will be with you."

Discuss:

Q: How could this be a "recipe" for self-control?

the Word

Read 2 Peter 1:4-8 together.

2 Peter 1:4-8

And because of his glory and excellence, he has given us great and precious promises. These are the promises that enable you to share his divine nature and escape the world's corruption caused by human desires.

In view of all this, make every effort to respond to God's promises. Supplement your faith with a generous provision of moral excellence, and moral excellence with knowledge, and knowledge with self-control, and self-control with patient endurance, and patient endurance with godliness, and godliness with brotherly affection, and brotherly affection with love for everyone.

The more you grow like this, the more productive and useful you will be in your knowledge of our Lord Jesus Christ.

a closer look

Read this box anytime to take a deeper look at the verses for this session.

One spice alone can be flavorful, but the true flavors are experienced when that spice is mixed with others and blended into food. Cinnamon alone isn't so great—but when it's mixed into a coffee cake...ahh! Delicious!

It's the same with self-control. It needs to be mixed with other "ingredients" to make our lives rich and flavorful. This passage gives us a "recipe" for success in the area of self-control. There's self-control—and the other "flavors" that go with it. Moral excellence. Knowledge. Patient endurance. Godliness. Brotherly affection. Love for everyone.

Mix these all together and what do you get? According to 2 Peter, we become more productive and useful in our knowledge of Jesus. We grow progressively and have zing, zest, and zip in our spiritual lives. Now that's flavorful!

scripture discussion questions

In groups of four or five, discuss these questions:

Q: Why do you think God recommends that self-control be added into our lives after moral excellence and knowledge? Why would self-control depend on those things being in place first?

Q: What about the order of the other things listed—what do you learn from the order these attributes are given?

Q: How can you add each of these things to your life? Be specific.

Q: What's the difference between the self-control required to resist temptation ("escape the world's corruption") and the self-control required to take healthy actions like exercising?

Q: How can you make a small turn in the direction of improving your physical and spiritual life in the next week? How can you keep yourself on course over the weeks and months to come?

tasty tip

Self-control is about more than just the ability to resist temptation. It's also about choosing to take actions that are beneficial to us. Physical exercise is an example. We know it benefits our bodies and helps us stay healthy. But we can't expect that exercising once a month will achieve results. It takes weekly practice, perseverance over the course of years, and resoluteness to start and maintain a healthy exercise program. We also train to be like God.

1 Timothy 4:7-8

"Train yourself to be godly. 'Physical training is good, but training for godliness is much better, promising benefits in this life and in the life to come.'"

What might this mean for your life?

Take Action

Let's not just *talk* about being resolute and following God's recipe for self-control, *let's do it!* Write below how you're going to develop perseverance and faithfulness in self-control, both in resisting temptation and in making healthy lifestyle choices this week. If you're having a hard time thinking of something, choose one of the ideas below. Next week, you'll share with one another how you did.

this week

○ I'm going to seek to follow God's recipe for developing self-control by:

....

....

....

....

○ I commit to adding one activity that incorporates both physical and spiritual training to my routine this week. I might try walking while listening to worship songs or praying while I'm lifting weights.

○ This week, I will use my spice mix to flavor a meal. Then I'll ask God to help me grow as described in 2 Peter 1:4-8. I want to add more "flavor" to my life!

○ When I face temptation this week, I'll stop and read Philippians 4:8-9 to help me focus my mind.

Prayer

End your time together in prayer to your Father.
Read Galatians 6:9:

> *So let's not get tired of doing what is good. At just the right time we will reap a harvest of blessing if we don't give up.*

When we lack self-control, we limit our ability to receive and experience the abundant life Jesus promised us—one full of the richest flavors of life! But as we practice self-control by following God's will, his Word, and his recipe for success, we'll be able to start tasting the richness of life!

Ask God to help you not feel weary in your pursuit of him. Pray to experience richness and blessing in the week ahead.

Girlfriend Time

Provide herb seeds (basil, cilantro, and chives are good choices) and starter pots, and have women plant a few seeds to take home and grow. Make this a fun, informal time for girlfriend-to-girlfriend conversation.

Consider how it takes time to grow self-control, and compare that to growing a plant. What's similar? What's different?

Still Thirsty?

If you're still thirsty to know more, check out these Scriptures.

James 1:12

"God blesses those who patiently endure testing and temptation. Afterward they will receive the crown of life that God has promised to those who love him."

Q: How does patient endurance relate to self-control? What does receiving a crown of life mean to you?

Proverbs 4:25-27

"Look straight ahead, and fix your eyes on what lies before you. Mark out a straight path for your feet; stay on the safe path. Don't get sidetracked; keep your feet from following evil."

Q: Where do you need this verse in your life right now? What is the safe path you need to be staying on? What can you fix your eyes on that will help you stay on the right path?

1 Thessalonians 4:1-8

"Finally, dear brothers and sisters, we urge you in the name of the Lord Jesus to live in a way that pleases God, as we have taught you. You live this way already, and we encourage you to do so even more. For you remember what we taught you by the authority of the Lord Jesus.

"God's will is for you to be holy, so stay away from all sexual sin. Then each of you will control his own body and live in holiness and honor—not in lustful passion like the pagans who do not know God and his ways. Never harm or cheat a Christian brother in this matter by violating his wife, for the Lord avenges all such sins, as we have solemnly warned you before. God has called us to live holy lives, not impure lives. Therefore, anyone who refuses to live by these rules is not disobeying human teaching but is rejecting God, who gives his Holy Spirit to you."

Q: What parts of this passage are meaningful to you? What guidance can you take from this that you can use this week?

James 1:2-4

"Dear brothers and sisters, when troubles come your way, consider it an opportunity for great joy. For you know that when your faith is tested, your endurance has a chance to grow. So let it grow, for when your endurance is fully developed, you will be perfect and complete, needing nothing."

Q: How can you consider troubles and temptations an opportunity for joy? How do endurance and self-control depend on each other to develop?

Psalm 1:1-3

"Oh, the joys of those who do not follow the advice of the wicked, or stand around with sinners, or join in with mockers. But they delight in the law of the Lord, meditating on it day and night. They are like trees planted along the riverbank, bearing fruit each season. Their leaves never wither, and they prosper in all they do."

Q: The strongest trees are the ones with the deepest roots, and they can withstand the worst of storms. How can you develop strong roots? How can self-control help you to become a tree that bears fruit in all the seasons of life?

My Reflections

My Reflections

Nourishing Freedom

Celebrating the Healthy Taste of Freedom

Note to the Hostess:

It's time to celebrate! Developing self-control in our lives frees us from being held captive by our self-indulgences, obsessions, and unhealthy desires so we're able to experience the abundant life Christ promised us. Create a party atmosphere for this session by decorating with balloons, streamers, and colorful tablecloths. Make special party "crowns" for women to recognize them for persevering in the study and running a good race!

Serve a variety of fruits to symbolize the harvest of the fruit of self-control women have developed over the course of the study. And don't forget the noisemakers—you'll want to make a loud and joyful noise to the Lord at the end of your time together!

Get It...Got It?...Good.

- snacks of fruit and something good to drink
- party décor
- 2 large trash cans or laundry baskets
- inflated balloons
- noisemakers

Mingling

Before you get into your celebration and study time, have women enjoy the snacks and talk about their week. Use these questions as discussion starters:

Q: How did you use your spice mix this week?

Q: What physical and spiritual training activity did you add to your routine?

Q: Share which ingredients you added to your life from God's recipe for developing self-control.

Before starting, pray something like this:

Thank you, God, for helping us to develop the fruit of self-control in our lives during our study together. We celebrate the taste of freedom we have experienced and ask to you continue to strengthen and nourish our dreams for the future. In Jesus' name, amen.

Experience

(Note: The hostess will prepare this experience)
You can't have a party without a party game! In this game women won't just have fun, they'll have fun with a purpose. It's silly but with a serious message about self-control.

Gather six volunteers to be your players. Designate the remaining women to be the "referees" of the game. Give each player one of the following instructions (be sure everyone hears these, as the referees will need to be keeping track):

• Player 1: You cannot scratch your nose.

- Player 2: You're not allowed to smile.

- Player 3: You can't move; you must remain perfectly still.

- Player 4: You can't blink.

- Player 5: You're not allowed to yell.

- Player 6: You can't run in circles.

Have your six players form two teams of three and stand facing each other. Each team has a trash can or laundry basket to the side. The object of the game is to keep the balloons in the air at all times. Any balloon that touches the ground will be put in the trash can of the team that let it drop. There are no other rules except the instructions they were given that they must follow throughout the game.

Instruct the "referees" to watch for possible violations of the rules. Start the game and the laughs by releasing 10 balloons, and keep playing until the last balloon drops!

At the end of the game, discuss:

Q: Which of the instructions were entirely unreasonable? What happened when the players tried to follow those instructions?

Q: How does this relate to setting unreasonable expectations for self-control?

Q: What about the easy-to-follow instructions? Can we set expectations too low? Is that a good or bad thing? Explain.

Q: What "rules" might God give us for how to maintain self-control in life? Are these reasonable or not? Explain.

the Word

Read John 4:6-7, 9-19, 25-26, and 28-30 together.

John 4:6-7, 9-19, 25-26, 28-30

Jacob's well was there; and Jesus, tired from the long walk, sat wearily beside the well about noontime. Soon a Samaritan woman came to draw water, and Jesus said to her, "Please give me a drink."

...The woman was surprised, for Jews refuse to have anything to do with Samaritans. She said to Jesus, "You are a Jew, and I am a Samaritan woman. Why are you asking me for a drink?" Jesus replied, "If you only knew the gift God has for you and who you are speaking to, you would ask me, and I would give you living water."

"But sir, you don't have a rope or a bucket," she said, "and this well is very deep. Where would you get this living water? And besides, do you think you're greater than our ancestor Jacob, who gave us this well? How can you offer better water than he and his sons and his animals enjoyed?"

Jesus replied, "Anyone who drinks this water will soon become thirsty again. But those who drink the water I give will never be thirsty again. It becomes a fresh, bubbling spring within them, giving them eternal life."

"Please, sir," the woman said, "give me this water! Then I'll never be thirsty again, and I won't have to come here to get water." "Go and get your husband," Jesus told her. "I don't have a husband," the woman replied. Jesus said, "You're right! You don't have a husband—for you have had five husbands, and you aren't even married to the man you're living with now. You certainly spoke the truth!"

"Sir," the woman said, "you must be a prophet...." The woman said, "I know the Messiah is coming—the one who is called Christ. When he comes, he will explain everything to us." Then Jesus told her, "I am the Messiah!"

...The woman left her water jar beside the well and ran back to the village, telling everyone, "Come and see a man who told me everything I ever did! Could he possibly be the Messiah?" So the people came streaming from the village to see him.

a closer look

Read this box anytime to take a deeper look at the verses for this session.

The Samaritan woman was thirsty, but because of her past, she could only go to the well to draw water when no one else was around. Her choices had separated her from others and from knowing Jesus. Yet when she went to get the water she was thirsty for, Jesus chose to meet her and offer her a drink of his living water—so she would never thirst again.

Despite her past, despite the sin, despite the rejection, despite anything, Jesus forgave this woman. She realized that Jesus knows everything about her and still extended grace. God's expectations were not only far from the expectations of others; they were far from her own expectations of herself. She immediately runs back to the village—to those who had rejected her—and shares the good news.

She had tasted freedom, been filled with living water, and couldn't wait to celebrate!

scripture discussion questions

In groups of four or five, discuss these questions:

Q: Beyond her physical thirst, what do you think the woman at the well was most thirsty for? What are you most thirsty for in life?

Q: Jesus accepted this woman as she was, even when others wouldn't. What does this teach you for your own life and your own struggles, especially in the area of self-control? What does it teach you as you relate to others?

Q: Jesus extended grace to the woman at the well. Do grace and self-control fit together? Explain.

Q: Imagine the freedom this woman suddenly felt. How are you now experiencing freedom as it relates to self-control?

Q: This woman had cause to celebrate and share her joy. What are you celebrating? How are you sharing your joy?

tasty tip

Psalm 37:4

"Take delight in the Lord, and he will give you your heart's desires."

How do we do this? Love God with all your heart, give him your heart and all your human appetites, and ask him to change your desires—so *your* heart's desires are *his* heart's desires!

Take Action

Let's not just *talk* about celebrating the taste of freedom of self-control, *let's do it!* Write below how you're going to delight in the Lord and pray for him to give you your heart's true desires in the next week. If you're having a hard time thinking of something, choose one of the ideas below.

this week

○ In the days and months ahead, I'm going seek grace and freedom by:

....

....

....

....

○ This week I will write down any unrealistic expectations I have of myself related to self-control and spend time asking God to help me find places I need to give myself grace.

○ I want to celebrate without letting go of self-control, so I'm going to choose a new activity to try and step into that with excitement and anticipation.

○ To celebrate the freedom I've tasted as I've developed the fruit of self-control in my life, I'll share my joy with supportive family and friends.

Prayer

End your time together in prayer to your Father.
Read and pray Colossians 1:9-12 together:

> So we have not stopped praying for you since we first heard about you. We ask God to give you complete knowledge of his will and to give you spiritual wisdom and understanding. Then the way you live will always honor and please the Lord, and your lives will produce every kind of good fruit. All the while, you will grow as you learn to know God better and better. We also pray that you will be strengthened with all his glorious power so you will have all the endurance and patience you need. May you be filled with joy, always thanking the Father. He has enabled you to share in the inheritance that belongs to his people, who live in the light.

It may be the end of your study together, but you're only just beginning to taste the freedom of self-control in your lives! Thank God for all he has done in the lives of the women during this study, and pray for them to continue to cultivate the fruit of self-control in their lives and be strengthened by God to run the race to victory!

Girlfriend Time

Since this is your last session, spend time just having fun and celebrating together. Play board games or have organized party games, play upbeat music and honor each woman for completing the study. Give fruit or fruit-inspired inexpensive gifts as awards for developing the fruit of self-control in their lives.

Before women leave, pass out noisemakers and ask everyone to "make a joyful noise" to the Lord in celebration of all he's done these past six weeks!

Still Thirsty?

If you're still thirsty to know more, check out these Scriptures.

2 Timothy 2:22

"Run from anything that stimulates youthful lusts. Instead, pursue righteous living, faithfulness, love, and peace. Enjoy the companionship of those who call on the Lord with pure hearts."

Q: Why is it important to *run* from things that stimulate lusts of the flesh? How can friendships with other believers help you with self-control?

1 John 2:15-17

"Do not love this world nor the things it offers you, for when you love the world, you do not have the love of the Father in you. For the world offers only a craving for physical pleasure, a craving for everything we see, and pride in our achievements and possessions. These are not from the Father, but are from this world. And this world is fading away, along with everything that people crave. But anyone who does what pleases God will live forever."

Q: List the things in the world that you crave. Next to each one, list a dream or desire you have for more of God in your life. How do the worldly cravings "fade" in comparison?

Romans 13:14

"Instead, clothe yourself with the presence of the Lord Jesus Christ. And don't let yourself think about ways to indulge your evil desires."

Q: How can the presence of the Lord be like clothing? How will "wearing" Jesus every day help you resist self-indulgence? What piece of your clothing can you use to help remind you to put on his presence every day?

John 15:1-4

"I am the true grapevine, and my Father is the gardener. He cuts off every branch of mine that doesn't produce fruit, and he prunes the branches that do bear fruit so they will produce even more. You have already been pruned and purified by the message I have given you. Remain in me, and I will remain in you. For a branch cannot produce fruit if it is severed from the vine, and you cannot be fruitful unless you remain in me."

Q: How has God "pruned" you during this study so you can produce more of the fruit of self-control in your life? What will you do to stay connected to Jesus?

Philippians 3:13-14

"No, dear brothers and sisters, I have not achieved it, but I focus on this one thing: Forgetting the past and looking forward to what lies ahead, I press on to reach the end of the race and receive the heavenly prize for which God, through Christ Jesus, is calling us."

Q: Why is it important for you to forget the past and look forward to what lies ahead in your life? What is the "heavenly prize" that will keep you motivated to persevere in resisting temptations and giving in to human desires?

My Reflections

My Reflections

STONECROFT® MINISTRIES

Stonecroft Ministries equips and encourages women of every age, every stage, and every face to positively impact their communities with the Gospel of Jesus Christ.

Our life-changing resources include:

- *Stonecroft Biblical Training Tools* including **AWARE** Evangelism (**A**lways **W**atching **A**nd **R**esponding with **E**ncouragement)

- Stonecroft *Bible Studies* guide participants simply, yet profoundly, into a rich relationship with the One who has so much to say to them

- Stonecroft Life Publications which clearly explain the Gospel message through stories of people whose lives have been impacted by Jesus Christ

- *Outreach groups* (such as Women's Connections, Moms on the Run, Vital Network, and Pray & Play) tailored to meet the needs of local communities

- *Regional and international training events* that equip women in evangelism, prayer, and leadership

- *Stonecroft's web site*, <u>stonecroft.org</u>, offering fresh content daily to equip and encourage you to impact your communities with the Gospel of Jesus Christ

Stonecroft Staff serve you via a dedicated and enthusiastic Home Office team, plus **Field Directors** stationed across America, overseeing the leadership of tens of thousands of dedicated volunteers who positively impact their communities for God and for good.

Contact us at <u>connections@stonecroft.org</u> or 800.525.8627 and visit <u>stonecroft.org</u> to learn more about these and other outstanding Stonecroft resources, groups, and events.

Women connecting with God, each other, and their communities
stonecroft.org